THE DORM CEO

*10 Steps to Finding and Launching
a Business While Enrolled in College*

THE DORM CEO

*10 Steps to Finding and Launching
a Business While Enrolled in College*

TERREL "T-TIME" DAVIS

Ordering Information:

Orders by U.S. trade bookstores and wholesalers. Quantity sales. Special discounts are available on quantity purchases by corporations, associations, and others. For details, contact the publisher at the following email address: **terrel@hbcuseed.com**

Connect with Terrel "T-Time" Davis:
Instagram: @Mr.ttime93
Facebook: @Terrel T-Time Davis

ISBN: 978-1-7366298-0-2

THANK YOU

for Purchasing The Dorm CEO by Terrel "T-Time" Davis!

Please scan the code below to get a

FREE Business Action Plan Checklist!

Scan here to access:

FREE GIFT

@hbcuseed | @mr.ttime93
www.hbcuseed.com

TERREL "T-TIME"
DAVIS

ABOUT THE AUTHOR

Venture Capitalist | Serial Entrepreneur | Philanthropist

Terrel "T-Time" Davis was born to be an entrepreneur. Before he graduated from Oakwood University with a bachelor's degree in Accounting and Business Management, he started his first business, T-Time Management, a tax accounting firm. He has taken his passion for food, finances, and real estate and founded successful companies in various arenas. He loves to serve his community by creating new opportunities for budding entrepreneurs. During his downtime, you can find him flying planes, skating, and traveling.

DEDICATION

*To Lucille Madden, Lane Madden,
and Scott Wilson... I chased my dreams
because of you all.*

CONTENTS

INTRODUCTION

Starting a business is as simple as coming up with a solution and bringing it to the marketplace. I understand that there are a lot more things you need to consider if you want your idea to be a smashing or even moderate success. If you are a college student, whatever you do, do not sell yourself short! You have a lot of things working in your favor.

- Ask any 40-something-year-old. Youth is absolutely on your side and it is a gift that you should use to your advantage. This is your season to hustle and stack!
- As a student, you have access to a ridiculous number of resources and mentors. Who doesn't want to help a student be successful?
- You can quickly rally a team of helpers from an almost unlimited pool of brilliant minds - and it does not have to cost you a bundle.
- Your overhead is lower now than it will be after you leave college. If grants, loans, and parents are covering living expenses, use that to your success advantage!
- Get the mistakes out of the way early in life. The longer you have been playing the

entrepreneurial game, the more likely it is that you will build an enterprise that endures.

And these are just a few advantages to getting started now.

My Story

I share my story so that when you look at where I am today you will know that I came from humble beginnings. I grew up in the hood on the west side of Lexington, KY. We had 13 people living in my house - including my five sisters and two brothers. We were raised by our loving Sweetgranny. My eighth - and youngest - sibling lived down the street because we had different fathers. Just to give you an idea of how tight things were, my siblings and I stayed in a single bedroom in our house. Our beds were lined up around the walls in that room and we had to share a lot because we didn't have much. None of this stopped me from dreaming big.

I was in elementary school the first time I realized I was an entrepreneur. I had a pack of Now and Later candy and this girl behind me tapped me on the shoulder and asked to try one. She loved it so much she offered me a whole dollar for the pack. I had paid a quarter for it. Even though I didn't know the technical term at the time, I immediately recognized the value in the law of supply and demand. The kids at the school I attended did not have access to the same snack options I did because the population of my school was predominantly white. Therefore, the neighborhood did not have the same demand for products we consumed in the hood. I had my pick of Hot Cheetos, Now and Later, Lemonheads, and other dime store candies. This girl and others in the school never even heard of a Now and Later.

So, I took that dollar, and $4 of my own money, and bought more candy to bring to school. The next day, I sold out of all my candy. I did the same thing every day for a couple of weeks before I decided to expand my business. I gathered four of my siblings together in a room and held my first business meeting. I told my siblings that I would supply the candy and I wanted them to be my distributors at the different schools they each attended. They agreed!

I bought 60 count cases of candy from Walmart. I gave them to my siblings and each Friday we would sit down and talk about what inventory was selling and what wasn't. I did this for a year and made quite a bit of profit. I was a 6th grader heading to 7th grade and my money looked good.

During the summers, I had a lawn care business. I used the funds I had earned while selling candy to purchase a lawnmower and weed eater so I could cut grass. But, I had horrible allergies! I decided not to let allergies stop me because I knew I was a good talker and could seal deals. I recruited friends from my neighborhood to do the work and after they were done, I would come to pick up the cash. I was able to expand my business quickly this way. My entrepreneurial spirit was so strong that I used to snag my sister's drawings and sell them at school! She used to wonder what happened to her artwork and never knew that it was me who had taken them. When she finally caught on to what I was doing, my uncle made me pay her a percentage of everything I had sold.

I have to stop here and say that my grandmother was very influential in my entrepreneurial journey. I pretty much got my hustle from her. She had health problems, but she would still pick me up and drop me off at different worksites. Most importantly, she believed in me.

When I entered 8th grade, my two great uncles decided to take care of me because I was making some pretty bad life choices and they could see me headed down the wrong path. Eventually, I moved from Kentucky to Atlanta, Georgia to live with them.

While there, I continued to sell candy, but did not start my first legal business until after my junior year. I launched TD Management, a project management company. I also started Ticks Enterprise, a computer repair company. I had no computer skills but funneled business to my uncle who was specialized in that area. I would take a percentage of the repair fee and pay him the rest.

Although I spent my formative years warming up my talents, I got my first taste of what it felt like to be a real businessman when I began interning at the Atlanta Bar Association Summer Law Internship Program. The internship taught me all of the basic skills on how to be successful in the corporate law and business world. Additionally, I made many lifelong friends and mentors (shout out to Wade, Natasha, Nekia, and Mariana for leading that program). During my first year interning, I was the recipient of the John Jenkins Award. This award was life-changing and began the next phase of my entrepreneurial journey.

The award I received afforded me a 4-year internship with the law department at United Parcel Service, or UPS. I had a great supervisor named Shannon, and an amazing mentor named Darren Jones. While working there, I met a woman who created limited liability companies for UPS. She sat down with me and shared all the ins and outs of setting up the legal entities and I used that information to create my first formal company called T-Time Management, LLC. I funded my new company with the money I earned through TD Management and Ticks Enterprise. At that time, I was entering my freshman year at Oakwood University in Huntsville, Alabama.

During my second semester, I experienced the third major shift in my entrepreneurial journey. I was studying to be an accountant and I learned how to do taxes. I was preparing my taxes for the first time when I learned about the American Opportunity Tax Credit. I ended up earning a $1,000 refund because I was an independent college student. I started telling people about my refund and people were shocked! They began to ask me to do their taxes, - and I agreed - for $50 a pop. I made an extra $1,000 in income that year. My roommate, Quinn Taylor, gave me my first investment to grow T-Time Management. My suitemates Chad, James, and Johnny were the first members on my team to help me promote my business.

The following year, I served 30 more customers than before. The next year, I served 150 customers. My experience with T-Time Management was pivotal to my career and before I graduated 5 years later, I created a "T-Time Tax Tour" and hit 6-figures in my tax business. I contacted 2,000 universities and of those that responded, they paid my team to come and do the students' taxes at no charge. During each 2-day event, I also taught students about creating limited liability corporations, credit repair, and how to start their own businesses. I even had some of the faculty from my university working for me. We completed about 1,000+ tax returns that year! As you can imagine, this was a huge win and also a crazy "learn as you go" experience for me as a young entrepreneur.

Also, during my sophomore year at Oakwood University, I launched a second business called Rideversity. It was a cross between Uber and Cashapp. Users could input their driving schedule into the app and another user could "catch a ride" with them by entering payment. Users could do short or long trips. I thought the business would gain a lot of traction. That project had so much potential. I had grown the business to a point where I even had an institutional investor ready to plant a $500,000 seed. I began pitching a "mileage plan" to universities (instead of a meal plan, I created a rider mileage plan), but it all came crashing down when I was not able to bridge the liability insurance gap.

Insurance was out of my reach for this project and the investor slipped away. I share this because it's just as important to share the struggles as it is to discuss the wins. You just have to learn to pivot. During that venture, I met my lifelong business partner, Julian Waddell. I always say if you see me being a Superhero, then just know he is in my ear guiding me, just as Lucius Fox does for Batman.

So what did I do after that disappointment? I turned Rideversity into a party bus and limo company! Oh, the stories I could tell about this venture! I will just say that the combination of the new Rideversity and T-Time Tax Service, helped me earn a living after graduation and beyond.

In 2018, I entered the restaurant business. I applied to different franchises including Chick-Fil-A, American Deli, Bojangles and Subway. While I was considering my options, my aunt came to my office and told me about a popular chef named Darnell Fergusen. He happened to be from Louisville, KY which is close to where I grew up in Lexington. The name of his restaurant was Super Chefs. I arranged for my friend Jordan Lobbins to drive me to Louisville so that I could meet with Darnell about investing in his company. We decided to form a partnership where we would be co-owners of any restaurant I could locate and fund. In my last pitch-meeting of the year, I secured a deal that was more than one million dollars. We re-named the brand Superhero Chefs, which now boasts a restaurant and food truck, with more to come.

From there, my partners Janna Peterson, Julian Waddell and I launched HBCU Seed, a venture capital and private equity fund. We were inspired to do this because it was so hard to find funding when we tried to launch businesses while in college. By starting our own investment company, we now had a way to give back to student entrepreneurs entering Historically Black Colleges and Universities. I also have an angel investment club called T-Time Capital. We fund businesses that are seeking less than $100,000.

I'm still at the beginning of my entrepreneurial journey and I hope my story inspires you to get started, stay focused and never quit. Your dreams are worth pursuing!

Let's get it!

Terrel "T-Time" Davis
Founder T-Time Management,
Co-Founder HBCU Seed,
Co-Founder Superhero Chefs

START NOW NOT LATER

The one thing I would like you to take from this book is found in a quote by Mark Twain who said, "The secret to getting ahead is getting started." Many people I speak with want to start "when the timing is right" or they are waiting for some life-defining "perfect moment." If you are reading this book, then I can say with certainty: you have inside of you the little pull that will make you put action steps behind your ideas - even if it means doing it afraid.

As a young person, it can probably feel like you have more time than you know what to do with. Thirty feels forever away, but it sneaks up quicker than you would think. Why not be strategic and *maximize* time while it's on your side? Here's what I mean.

Your focus might be on finishing college, and that in itself is a huge accomplishment. Your other focus might be on having a social life which is super common as a young person! I'm not here to judge! I believe that you can do well in school, have a modest social life and start growing a business that might even pay you more than your first post-college job. Why does this even matter? Let me drop a few stats on you.

Student Loan Debt

Listen, student loans out here in these streets are no joke! The non-profit economic news organization, *Marketplace*, posted an article stating that a whole 70% of y'all will leave college with some debt. On average, that is about $30K in debt[1]. Imagine trying to pay for your car, insurance, first apartment, food, bills, social life then - BOOM - 6 months later, your student loan payments kick in at an extra $450 a month. Honestly, a lot of people who return to college for another degree (and more debt), depend on their parents (which isn't fair to them), or get their student loans deferred for the next 36 months.

Make Money

You can make some serious money. Although I like to get inspiration from CEOs who did this in a big way (Bill Gates, Mark Zuckerberg, etc.), I am most inspired by those who are more relatable. Take Seth Berkowitz who baked Insomnia Cookies while a student at UPenn. They were so popular, he now has 65 locations serving up his company's cookies. His business was booming before he even graduated. I assure you, Berkowitz is definitely making more than the average 2019 college graduate, who pulled around $51K[2] that year. However, in 2019, the job outlook was better than it had been in the 12 previous years! I think you can agree that the job market in 2021 and beyond is pretty unpredictable.

Avoid Delayed Graduation Dates

The global impact of the pandemic spawned by the rapid spread of Covid-19, has changed the global market in ways most students (and non-students!) didn't see coming. This is where traditional and non-traditional students have been heavily impacted due to a loss of financial aid, on-campus housing and side income opportunities. As such, an additional income can help supplement the drop in the financial sources that used to be more readily available.

Uncertain Job Outlook

The pandemic has also created a movement towards more contract work, work-from-home opportunities and virtual jobs. This shift has caused some businesses to thrive while others have had to close their doors. What if the degree path you currently hold is on the decline in the coming years? Or, what if your career choice is in high demand? Why not squeeze everything you can out of both scenarios by growing a side hustle?

Develop Real-World Experience

Richard Branson, the founder of Virgin Records, once said that entrepreneurship is like a roller coaster - messy and chaotic. Having business experience can make it less messy and chaotic. It makes sense to get as much experience as possible, as early in life as possible. For example, when I was still a student, I landed an internship that taught me how to launch limited liability companies. With that knowledge and experience, I began to get paid for using my new skills to help my peers launch their businesses.

Access to Mentors & Resources

I will go into more detail about this in later steps, but this gem deserves an early mention. Getting a mentor early in your business gives you access to info that can save you time and dollars. Lucky for you, mentors love to take college students under their wing. Can you see the benefits of developing a solid relationship with a successful business leader who can help you avoid costly mistakes as you build your own business?

T-Time Tip

"YOUR PASSION WILL BE THE THING THAT GETS YOU UP IN THE MORNING. IT WILL BE THE SAME THING THAT KEEPS YOU UP AT NIGHT. BE SURE TO LET IT MOTIVATE YOU, BUT DON'T LET YOUR PASSION CAUSE YOU TO MAKE MISTAKES THAT YOU COULD HAVE AVOIDED HAD YOU ALSO PLANNED FOR SUCCESS.

FIND YOUR BUSINESS IDEA

I hope I have convinced you that now is your time to start your entrepreneurial journey! Before you let the waves of business options leave you feeling confused about your next step, I got you! In this chapter, you will find a list of business ideas that I selected because they are sustainable, profitable, and scalable. But as a starting point, you want to select your business idea based on your personal interests, personality, and consumer demand. Then ask yourself, do people even want what I'm trying to sell?

If you don't already know what type of business to start, there are a lot of business idea-generating tools available online that you can access with very little effort. This section will focus on four types of businesses. The goal of the examples on these lists is to get your ideas flowing. The types of businesses I will discuss are Online, Product Based, Service Based, and Food Based. Keep in mind that some of the categories may overlap.

T-Time Tip

Always have a backup plan just in case your business takes a while to produce money. You need a way to keep surviving until your business starts to thrive.

Online Business

A lot of businesses fall under this category which includes any product or service-based opportunity that has a web-based presence. There are two types. Service and information-based products, or e-commerce. Here are a few examples of businesses you could launch exclusively online:

- Clothing Boutique
- E-books and Courses
- Drop Shipping
- Writing/Editing
- Art and Design
- Social Media
- Teaching
- Web Development
- Tech Support
- Virtual Assistant

Product Based

A product-based business involves selling an actual physical product. Products can include a variety of items from hats, clothing, books, custom Jordans, jewelry and handmade items to equipment, tools, and anything that the seller can find a market to sell.

- Apparel
- Gadgets
- Inventions
- White Label Products
- Jewelry
- Customizable Products

Service-Based

If you want to launch a business in this category, look at the skills you currently have and think of ways to monetize them. If you have excellent relationship building, problem-solving, and communication skills and you enjoy frequent contact with customers, this category can be a great fit for you.

- Childcare
- Coaching
- Tax Preparation
- Real Estate
- Health and Fitness Trainer
- Notary Services
- Bookkeeping
- Editing
- Tutoring
- College Test Prep
- Marketing Strategist
- Temporary Housing Rentals

Food-Based

A food-based enterprise can be as simple as selling cookies and desserts or as complex as contracting a lab to formulate protein shakes or vitamin capsules. Your start-up investment cost, time available, and access to regulated food prep spaces will guide your decisions.

- Baked Goods
- Food Truck
- Nutritional Supplements
- Food Prep
- Catering
- Fresh Pressed Juices
- Desserts
- Charcuterie Boards

T-Time Tip

It's okay to start one business to raise capital for the other business you want to launch. For example, you could sell food prep meals for *right now* money and use your profits to save up for the deposit on your food truck.

STEP THREE

BECOME LEGIT

It is not as difficult as one might think to legally start a business. Here are two steps you can take to quickly graduate from having a hobby or idea into launching a legit business.

1. Research - Find out what you need to know before you get started

Before you jump in the ring, you will want to do some basic research. Find out who your competition is and how you will reach your target market What will you name your company? Will you have an LLC, sole proprietorship, corporation, non-profit, or any other business structure? Where will you find funding and a location? Even if you are working from home, you need to know whether your city and county have certain zoning restrictions for the type of business you want to start.

T-Time Tip

Your business is a solution to a bunch of people's problems. If what you want to offer the world doesn't solve problems keep brainstorming until you come up with something that does!

A business plan is at the root of your investigation. It will help you answer these questions and more. Do not overcomplicate the process. Keep your plan simple and add to it as you learn more and expand your business idea. One of the best ways to keep it simple is by using a business plan template. Use Google to find one for your industry. Always know that you do not have to fill in every single section of the traditional business plan. Fill in the sections that give your idea clarity and direction. At the end of the chapter and in the bonuses at the back of the book, there are links and QR codes for the resources that will help you get started and follow through on everything discussed in this section.

2. Taxes and banking give you the legal credentials you need to do business

Now you will need to secure your tax identification number, which is available on the IRS.gov website, linked below. This ID is called an Employee Identification Number (EIN) and you will need it to file taxes, open business accounts, and get a resale certificate (needed for selling items).

You will also want to go to your city or county's website and apply for your business license. You may have to do this in person at City Hall. Once you have that, you will also register your business with your state's department of revenue. That's where you will pay your sales tax according to your state's schedule. To easily locate the proper authority for where you plan to set up your business Google "[Your State] + Department of Revenue + Business Tax."

Now that you have your business name, legal structure, and EIN, you can open your business banking account. This step not only opens up an official line of business credit, but it will also help you keep your personal and business finances separate. You will thank me later for that!

Employer Id Numbers | Internal
Revenue Service

Get Your Employee ID Number (it's free!)
Internal Revenue Service (IRS) - https://www.irs.gov/businesses/small-businesses-self-employed/employer-id-numbers.

T-Time Tip

I tried to keep this section as simple as possible because I want to help you get rid of any excuses you might have about why you cannot start a business. Get to the bottom of why you think you cannot do this, and cancel that line of thinking!

YOUR MISSION MATTERS!

Understand your mission by answering a few questions:

1

WHAT DO WE DO?

2

HOW ARE WE GONNA DO IT?

3

WHO ARE WE DOING IT FOR?

4

WHAT VALUE DO WE BRING TO THE TABLE?

VISIT OUR WEBSITE FOR MORE:

HBCUSEED.COM

STEP FOUR

IDENTIFY AND FOCUS ON YOUR PRIORITIES

Prioritize

Discovering your priorities can be a challenge. When you break it down into steps, it's easier to figure out. First, determine your short-term and long-term career goals and how school fits into them. Questioning the reasons for both your school and business decisions can help you determine the most important priorities.

Ask yourself these four questions:

1. Why am I starting a business before graduation?
2. Why do I value staying in school?
3. Can my schoolwork help me build a business?
4. Do I see a future career with my business after graduation?

When answering these questions, clearly expand on your responses. Once you know your *why*, you can then decide when to sacrifice study time versus business opportunities. Each situation depends on the urgency of deadlines, but setting priorities can help give clarity about which goal to focus on at any given moment.

T-Time Tip

Don't beat yourself up if you want to work on a business strategy for a few days. If you want to integrate your class plan into your business plan, make sure you implement some of the key lesson strategies into your business or networking endeavors for the week.

Choose the Right Courses

If you are concerned about making good grades, it is okay to bridge the gap between school and work. Choose your major and electives carefully. Select ones that help you to be strategic. You want to be able to network with experts, professors, and people who have the same mindset as you. Besides, if your business is related to your major, you will save yourself a crazy amount of time and effort!

T-Time Tip

Take a for-credit independent study course for a semester or quarter. This allows you to focus on research for your business. During another semester, take a project-based entrepreneurship class to gain experience creating prototype designs for products and/ or strategy or marketing development for your business.

Utilize School Resources

You are already paying for access to your school's career center, counselors, and other resources. Take full advantage of all the tools located in different departments. Think about the printing services, free wifi, online resources and library. As a student, you have access to deep discounts on everything from books, software, and services. When you graduate, these things will be less convenient and more expensive, so get it while you can!

T-Time Tip

If your college has a writing center, take advantage of it for promotional materials and collaborate with student organizations to help promote your business. You can also book conference rooms for meeting space.

Schedule and Checklists

Taking on the challenge of school work and launching a business is a lot of work, so you will need a solid way to stay up with all the details. One of the best things I can share with you is the power of managing your time as if you are already a successful CEO.

If you like structure, you can use project management software like Asana, Trello, or Monday to keep track of your tasks, make lists, and communicate with your team. If you prefer a simpler process, a good old-fashioned planner, whiteboard, or calendar will work, too.

You can block out chunks of time for studying and business activities. Or you can choose to work your business only on certain days of the week.

T-Time Tip

Regardless of what style of schedule you choose, when you are working your business - be about business! Always do the tasks that will make you money, close the deal, or lead to a sale - first.

BUILD YOUR BUSINESS BUDGET

Building a startup will truly be one of the hardest things you will do. Yet chasing your passion, making an impact, and making a profit are all worth the struggle. But, first things first. You need to know how much the different parts of your business will cost you. With that information, you will know how much money you will need to earn each week to keep operations running. Once you know what your expenses are, you can build your marketing efforts. After all, you have to learn how much product or services you need to sell to pay your bills. What is left over is either going towards getting more clients (marketing!) or it's money in the bank.

Budget Basics

Know your current money situation. You are probably young and almost famous, so assets such as personal goods, stocks, income and real estate are unlikely to be significant. You are a college student! Join the club and don't feel bad about it. We all started at zero. Okay, well, most of us start at zero. I know I did.

Here are 5 steps to putting together a budget, fast:

1. List all your income sources for your business. How does your company make money? Write

those down and add them up. Do not leave anything out.

2. List all of the expenses that will not change. There are certain bills that you can always expect to be there. Examples include rent, utilities, monthly provider fees (Zoom, Shopify, automated email service, phone, etc.). These are your fixed expenses. It is okay to add in expenses that you know will come up soon. Take a look at your bank statement so you don't miss anything. Write them down and add everything up.

3. List all of your expenses that have amounts that change from month to month. Your electric bill, gas, shipping fees, product re-orders, etc. are considered variable expenses. Look at a couple of month's worth of bank statements to get an idea of what you should prepare for. Write them down and add them up.

4. List those expenses that likely only happen one time per year. Your website hosting fees, attorney fee, laptop, heat press machine, commercial mixer, other equipment, etc. Anticipate the expense, and write it down so you can plan for it.

5. Put it all together to create a picture of what your income and expenses might look like in future months. Let's see it in action!

Sample Income and Expenses Exercise

INCOME

Client Hourly Earnings: $5,000
Product Sales: $1,500
Online Sales: $2,200
Loans: $800
Savings: $700
Investment Income: $200
Total Income: $10,400

EXPENSES

Fixed
Rent: $630
Internet: $89
Website hosting: $50
Insurance: $112
Government and bank fees: $20
Cell phone: $98
Legal services: $118
Total Fixed Costs: $1,117

Variable
Sales commissions: $1350
Contractor wages: $380

Electricity bill: $176
Gas bill: $75
Water bill: $125
Printing services: $180
Raw materials: $612
Travel and events: $0
Transportation: $64
Total Variable Expenses: $2,962

One-Time Spends
Office furniture: $450
Office supplies for a new location: $1,400
New client tracking software: $500
Client gifts: $100
Mastermind membership: $997
Total One-Time Spends: $3,447

Total Expenses: $7,526

**Total Income ($10,400) – Total Expenses ($7,526)
= Total Net Income ($2,874)**

T-Time Tip

It is much easier to track your income and expenses if you use bookkeeping software like FreshBooks or QuickBooks. There are a ton of YouTube videos about how to use these resources. Or for a fee, you can just send your receipts to a bookkeeper who can manage them for you.

STEP SIX

BUILD YOUR TEAM

business development offices or experts in the field. As a student, most people are generally willing to help you. Mentors are there to offer sage advice, coaching, and opportunities to connect with businesses for college credit.

T-Time Tip

Use platforms like Envelop, Mogul, FledgeWing or the Small Business Administration to connect with local mentors, or to find capital.

Employees

You may have chosen a business model that requires you to hire employees who will help fulfill the client demand for your product or service. If that sounds like you, consider temporary employees who can be found through websites like Indeed.com, Monster.com, ZipRecruiter.com, CraigsList.com and Upwork.

com. Do not forget that LinkedIn is another resource if you're looking to connect with quality potential hires. Automated texting services are another opportunity to get in immediate contact with potential employees. Make use of this technology for a competitive advantage.

Advisory Board

This is an informal board that is not legally attached to your company, but members provide you with strategies, advice, and support with hiring, marketing, and growth. There are no hard rules about how to meet with your advisory board, but you want to choose individuals who have a proven track record. In consideration of their busy schedules, you can meet with them individually or schedule video or phone conference calls. When trying to sell someone about the benefits of being on your board, be patient and willing to follow up, follow up, and follow up again. Humility is everything because you need them more than they need you!

T-Time Tip

Look to build a network of peers and employees who are smarter and more skilled than you. Make sure they share your vision and that you stay open to their feedback and advice.

When You Should Hire Employees

- Brand Ambassadors
- In-person events
- Seasonal work
- Filling an existing employee gap

BETA TEST YOUR PRODUCT OR SERVICES

Customers First

Listen, I cannot emphasize this enough. If you are not making sales, you do not have a valid business. As an angel investor, one of the biggest mistakes I have observed new entrepreneurs make is becoming stuck in the hype of "build it and they will come." That's just not the case. You have got to get out there and sell customers on your big idea and make sure they want it before you spend a lot of money and time on product creation. So, sell the heck out of your product or service first.

Cheap Prototypes Rule

Here is an example. If you are starting a t-shirt business, use free mockup software to showcase your designs and post those mockups to social media to generate customer interest and orders. If you have another type of product, you can also create a brochure that lists all the selling points of your product. Put the professionally designed image inside the brochure and *BAM!* you have something to put in the hands of potential customers and investors. Connect with some of your peers or hit up a designer on www.fiverr.com who can make it look and smell like money. These are inexpensive options that attract your customers and limit how much you need to invest before your full product is available.

Did you know that James Dyson created 5,127 prototypes of the now famous Dyson vacuum cleaner many people know about today?

In fact, every single manufacturer in the U.S. completely rejected his work. In 1995, the product became a huge success in the UK. Guess what though? Dyson began building his prototypes in 1979!

The company eventually developed five different types of vacuums and expanded their market to include air treatment products, hair styling tools, lighting solutions, air hand dryers and other tools.

This is an example of the entrepreneurial mindset and also a reminder to never give up!

Sales Page

You are going to need a hub where prospects can read up about your product and company and also where customers can place an order or contact you. You can design and create a simple website on Wix.com or Shopify.com that follows the same outline as the brochure. Include a video that discusses the product and company vision. You also want to have a way that customers can sign up for your email list. Give them something to click because it does mimic real life buying behavior. I like MailChimp.com and OntraPort.com as options for automated email services.

T-Time Tip

Install Google Analytics or Crazyegg.com on your site to track page views, clicks, and other useful data that will give you information about how consumers are interacting with your product online.

STEP EIGHT

FIND FUNDING

Financial growth is an important factor in the early stages of any business. If you are looking to generate money flow, college is a great place to find funding sources for your startup. Finance and scholarship offices can help you secure loans, federal grants, scholarships, and fellowships that offer students financial assistance. Holding an email address ending with ".edu" is lucrative because there are specific funding options available for student entrepreneurs. Just be sure to confirm that any bills covered by actual student loans are qualifiable living expenses! Let's look at some funding opportunities that may support your small business or at least cover your personal expenses while you grow your business.

How Much Money Do You Need?

In order to get the best funding options, you must build your budget as outlined in **Step 5** of this book. Please refer to the refillable income and expenses worksheet in **Bonus 2** towards the end of this book, as well.

Venture Capital

Self-funding is not always an option for a lot of college entrepreneurs. However, an outside investor or investors may often see a fast-growing company like yours as an opportunity to further a good cause, instigate social change or just get a moderate or high return on their investment. Do some research to make sure you are linking up with a solid company, with a good reputation. Prepare for the angel investor or firm to do some serious due diligence on your company including the employees, products, and services. But the benefit to all the paperwork is you will have an experienced addition to your team that has a vested interest in your success.

Business Loans

You can get a business loan through a local or online bank or even the Small Business Administrative Agency. Start with the bank where you opened your business account and search other banks from there.

Crowdfunding

This is an exciting opportunity for accessing large amounts of capital even if your credit is not the best or if you cannot quite meet the scrutiny of the investment or traditional banker. You might even feel more confident about taking larger sums of money because the risk is spread out over a lot more people. Real talk: If your crowdfunding campaign takes off, that means you have proof that people will indeed buy into your concept. That looks really good if, or when, you decide to approach angel investors or venture funding sources.

Scan this code to get funding for your business!

Scan here to access:

GET FUNDING

@hbcuseed | @mr.ttime93
www.hbcuseed.com

T-Time Tip

Crowdsourcing offers unique funding opportunities. This method is now helping to generate startup revenue and draws attention from businesses and investors. While you are still in college, reach out to a large and unique school community to promote your business or product. You could even create a crowdsourcing event on your campus.

SOFT LAUNCH VS. HARD LAUNCH AND THE RE-LAUNCH

You have done the hard work. You know what your audience wants, you know what it will cost and you have a brochure or prototype of your product. You are ready to launch! You may have done everything right up until this point, but let's keep the proper business perspective. The Harvard Business Review found that more than 70% of product launches fail [4]. Understanding this can help you get back up to try again, and again, and yet again because sometimes that is what it takes to win. Let's talk about the benefits of doing a soft launch vs. a hard launch.

Benefits of a Soft Launch

A *soft launch* is when you release your beta product without much fanfare or marketing. You sell at a discounted price and continue to make tweaks as you learn from your user's experience.

- Your reputation doesn't get trashed if the product doesn't meet expectations.
- You can save "boo koo" money because it doesn't cost as much as a full launch.
- You can slowly roll out new features of your product so that customers stay engaged.
- You can quickly cancel and regroup if feedback is not favorable.

3 Reasons Launches Flop:

1. There isn't a market for the product or service
2. The company can't support the insane demand
3. The product is based on a fad or trend, so it's short lived

- This is the strategy for you if you know your product is ready for a full rollout, but you would like sales, engagement, and feedback.

T-Time Tip

Carefully monitor social media and anywhere users would likely post reviews for your product. Paying attention to the user response helps you to compile information for tweaks you may need to make.

Benefits of a Hard Launch

A *hard launch* is when you run out of the gate with the biggest bang you can make. You have full marketing on board, grand opening, a community-wide or even the global release of your product or service.

- You will grab a lot of publicity because you are doing something that generates attention.
- You will probably get paid more money, faster because you will have a flood of new users.
- Your focused marketing strategy makes reaching ideal customers easier.
- When you go big, you overshadow the competition.
- This is the move to make if you have a solid product, worked out the kinks, and expect a high level of success.

So, which launch type is best for you? Whether you take your launch in baby steps or go big, ultimately, most companies have to work out a few kinks to re-launch an updated version of a product.

The Re-Launch

If sales or reviews were not as expected, you will need to make some changes before you push your product back into the world. This era of Covid has proven it is not the time to do the same old thing you did last time. Customers want deeper connections and, let's face it, competition is fierce out in these digital streets.

Begin by getting a plan together and make sure to poll employees, customers, and even your vendors about what they have observed, and what needs to change. Now is not the time to go quiet on social media. Instead, keep producing valuable content and engaging with customers and potential customers via email and whatever platform they use most. Put out well-branded digital content and market, market, market your upgraded product.

T-Time Tip

Have a plan in place for how you will handle a crisis should it come up. Run through scenarios with your team so that at the key moment, you are ready, rather than wasting time getting ready.

OPERATE, SCALE, AND EXIT STRATEGY

Every enterprise navigates key phases after launching or relaunching. Business owners start and maintain standard operations, the business experiences growth and, eventually, the owner exits the company. I have experienced each of these phases in every company I ever launched, including the candy business I started when I was in 6th Grade. Let's look at each piece and I will share some examples.

Operate

These are the activities you perform every day to produce, sell, and distribute your products or services. You will have administrative tasks like making calls, filing, scheduling, organizing, and managing inventory. You may also spend time managing social media, creating digital content, and serving customers. You will have to communicate with your team, contractors, and those who provide services for your physical location. As a business owner, marketing and generating revenue are some of the most critical tasks you will perform. Spend most of your daily time doing Income Producing Activities (IPA). These are the tasks most directly related to making sales and marketing your business.

DON'T: If you start a mobile massage company, for example, spend most of your time posting on social media and growing your following. Spend any other available time serving the clients who book your services. If you don't have time to book new clients and market your business - uh oh! You need to re-evaluate the percentage of time you spend on Income Producing Activities (IPA).

DO: Instead, spend most of your time booking new and existing appointments and selling products like oils or massage tools. Next, you would be placing ads, booking vendor booths, and posting marketing material online and at locations where your customers hang out. You would be creating events where you can get bookings for your services and also make product sales. Then you make room for everything else! If you are so busy booking clients and selling products that you don't have time to do other tasks well - congratulations! You are ready to move to the next phase, which is to scale your business.

T-Time Tip

Regularly create a Profit and Loss statement using your accounting software. This statement will tell you if you are selling enough products and services to become profitable. If you are not, take a look at how much of your daily operations involve active marketing and closing sales. Do more!

Scale

So, why are you scaling your business? What is it you are trying to achieve? Keep your end goal in mind because it will guide *how* to scale. Regardless of what your endgame is, every new business must scale operations to become profitable as soon as possible. Scaling involves hiring staff or contractors and outsourcing Non-Income Producing Activities like design, administrative duties, advertising, accounting, and other activities. You may need to upgrade your systems and platforms to accommodate more clients. If you are a digital course provider, you might need to upgrade to the pro version. If you have an online boutique, you may need to rent or buy a warehouse. If you have a realtor's office, you may need to hire a CFO or administrative/sales team to manage leads and conduct follow-up calls.

As a partner in a restaurant franchise, I scaled up by purchasing a food truck and by expanding to a new location. I have a goal in mind for how many franchise locations I want to launch each year. This requires me to create a plan that is attractive to investors. It takes cash to scale.

T-Time Tip

When you are ready to take on a larger customer load, but are not quite ready for full-time staff, consider hiring a virtual sales or administrative team through companies like Magic, WoodBows, UpWork or other sites.

From day one in my tax preparation business, I looked for ways to achieve our initial sales figures and to scale the operation. I budgeted for more staff and increased the operations budget. This meant more marketing, customer care, and growth for every aspect of the business.

Regardless of the business type, I never see my business venture as a means to an end. I know at some point I will move on and need a plan in place for how to exit the business. I discuss this further in the next section.

Exit Strategy

As a business owner, you should not only be thinking and planning for how you will make money from your business, but also how much you can make. There are many options to choose from. For example, with my candy selling business, I completely liquidated my inventory and moved on to the next venture. However, with the party bus and limo service, it was a bit more complex. I chose to donate the bus to a local church and the limo to a mental health non-profit organization. As part of my solid CEO exit strategy, I knew I wanted to funnel funds into another venture so that I could continue receiving consistent revenue. I also had to consider my contractors, informing customers, and also the sale of equipment.

But what about you? Will you sell your assets? Will you sell your company to a family member, investor, or possibly another business? Will you make it an Initial Public Offering (IPO)? There are pros and cons to each strategy. Here are questions you can explore to help you narrow down the approach that fits best. Then, explore your responses with a business mentor who can help you better understand the implications.

- How quickly do I want the cash out of my company?
- How much profit do I want to take?
- Do I still want to retain ownership in the company?
- How important is it to keep my company in the family?
- Will I start another business venture after this one?
- What other questions can you add to this list?

T-Time Tip

One of the keys to my many successes has been that I always use the funds from one venture to fund the next venture. I start and operate my business with the end goal in mind.

BONUS 1
50+ BUSINESS IDEAS

Grocery Store
Drive-In Movie Theater
Bank
Clothing Boutique
Car Repair Shop
Tow Truck Business
Candle Making
Nightclub
Car Dealership
Bottled Water
Security Guard
Convenience Store
Car Rental
Shoe Store
Micro-Lending Company
Health and Senior Services
Retail Consignments
Convenience Store
Information Technology
Candy & Comfort Food
Child Care / Day Care
Tattoo Parlors
Training and Tutoring Services
Teaching & Consulting Businesses
Web-Based Businesses

Writing & Editing Businesses

Digital Art & Design Businesses

Specialty Craft Businesses

Lifestyle Businesses

Cleaning & Maintenance

eCommerce Businesses

Art & Design Businesses

Writing & Editing Businesses

Social Media Businesses

Marketing Businesses

Teaching & Consulting Businesses

Data Collection & Transcription Businesses

Tech Businesses

Landscaping

Community Garden

Green Beauty

Green Cleaning

Gourmet Popcorn

Family Restaurant

Food Truck

Hot Sauce

Meals to Go

Dog Walking

Construction

Painting

Decorating

Tour Bus

Sightseeing Tours

BONUS 2
FILLABLE START-UP BUDGET WORKSHEET

Use a template for an Excel Spreadsheet or see the References and Resources for a link and QR code to a refillable budget sheet courtesy SBA.gov

My Company Name
Best T-Shirt Startup Overview

STARTUP OVERVIEW		Budget		Actual		(Under) / Over
Total Expenses	$	34,100.00	$	45,000.00	$	10,900.00
Administrative / General	$	1,200.00	$	900.00	$	(300.00)
Location / Office	$	7,200.00	$	6,800.00	$	(400.00)
Marketing	$	1,200.00	$	3,400.00	$	2,200.00
Labor	$	24,000.00	$	32,000.00	$	8,000.00
Other	$	500.00	$	1,900.00	$	1,400.00
Total Funding	$	24,200.00	$	27,950.00	$	3,750.00
Investors	$	1,200.00	$	1,650.00	$	450.00
Loans	$	17,000.00	$	19,500.00	$	2,500.00
Additional Funding	$	6,000.00	$	6,800.00	$	800.00
Funding Less Expenses	$	(9,900.00)	$	(17,050.00)	$	(7,150.00)

STARTUP FUNDING		Budget		Actual		(Under) / Over
Investors						
Owner 1	$	600.00	$	500.00	$	-
Owner 2	$	600.00	$	1,050.00	$	450.00
Owner 3	$	-	$	-	$	-
Other	$	-	$	-	$	-
Total	$	1,200.00	$	1,550.00	$	450.00
Loans						
Bank Loan	$	17,000.00	$	19,500.00	$	2,500.00
Non-Bank Loan	$	6,000.00	$	6,800.00	$	800.00
Other	$	-	$	-	$	-
Total	$	23,000.00	$	26,300.00	$	3,300.00
Additional Funding						
Grant	$	2,800.00	$	2,500.00	$	(300.00)
Other	$	3,200.00	$	4,300.00	$	1,100.00
Total	$	6,000.00	$	6,800.00	$	800.00

BONUS 3
ACTION PLAN
CHECKLIST

Scan the access code to get a step-by-step guide for how to start your business.

Scan here to access:

ACTION
PLAN

@hbcuseed | @mr.ttime93
www.hbcuseed.com

BONUS 4
ONE PAGE BUSINESS PLAN

Scan the code to access a one-page business plan template.

Scan here to access:

BUSINESS PLAN

@hbcuseed | @mr.ttime93
www.hbcuseed.com

NOTES

Use these pages to write your vision and make it plain ....

REFERENCES AND RESOURCES

1. Marketplace (2019). 70% of college students graduate with debt. How did we get here? https://www.marketplace.org/2019/09/30/70-of-college-students-graduate-with-debt-how-did-we-get-here/

2. SHRM (2019). Average Starting Salary for Recent College Grads Hovers Near $51,000. https://www.shrm.org/resourcesandtools/hr-topics/compensation/pages/average-starting-salary-for-recent-college-grads.aspx

3. Business Insider (2014). 6 Steps to Building a Successful Business in College. https://www.businessinsider.com/how-to-start-business-in-college-2014-2

4. Harvard Business Review (2011). Why Most Product Launches Fail. https://hbr.org/2011/04/why-most-product-launches-fail

5. How to Create a Business Budget for Your Small Business: https://www.justbusiness.com/finance/how-to-create-a-business-budget

6. **Calculate your Startup Costs:** https://www.sba.gov/business-guide/plan-your-business/calculate-your-startup-costs

7. **Get Tips for How to Write a Business Plan (scan the code):** https://www.sba.gov/business-guide/plan-your-business/write-your-business-plan#section-header-2

Write Your Business Plan
www.sba.gov

8. **Startup Costs Worksheet:** https://www.sba.gov/sites/default/files/2020-08/Startup%20Costs%20Worksheet-508.pdf

Thank you for ordering my book!
If you've had a great experience,
please consider leaving a review on
Amazon.com!

Made in the USA
Monee, IL
20 July 2024

61553185R10069